Fact Finders®

ADVENTURES ON THE AMERICAN FRONTIER

BOLD RIDERS

THE STORY OF THE PONY EXPRESS

BY JOHN MICKLOS, JR.

Consultant:
Richard Bell
Associate Professor of History
University of Maryland, College Park

CAPSTONE PRESS
a capstone imprint

Fact Finders are published by Capstone Press,
1710 Roe Crest Drive, North Mankato, Minnesota 56003
www.capstonepub.com

LIBRARY OF CONGRESS CATALOGING-IN-PUBLICATION DATA
Micklos, John.
  Bold riders: the story of the Pony Express / by John Micklos, Jr.
    pages cm. — (Fact finders. Adventures on the American frontier.)
  Summary: "Examines the history of the Pony Express, including why it formed, the dangers riders faced, and why its legend lives on today"—Provided by publisher.
  Includes bibliographical references and index.
  ISBN 978-1-4914-4896-0 (library binding)
  ISBN 978-1-4914-4910-3 (paperback)
  ISBN 978-1-4914-4928-8 (eBook PDF)
1. Pony express—History—Juvenile literature. 2. Postal service—United States—History—Juvenile literature. 3. West (U.S.)—History—1860–1890—Juvenile literature. I. Title.
  HE6375.P65M53 2016
  383'.18—dc23   2015007608

EDITORIAL CREDITS
Brenda Haugen, editor; Juliette Peters, designer; Tracy Cummins, media researcher; Laura Manthe, production specialist

PHOTO CREDITS
Bridgeman Images: Archives Charmet, 5, Peter Newark American Pictures, 23, 24; Capstone Press: 7; Corbis: CORBIS, 14, 25; Getty Images: Buyenlarge, 12-13, 27, E. P. Vollum/Hulton Archive, 9, Illustration by Ed Vebell, 18-19, Keystone, 6; Library of Congress: 10, 29; Newscom: Underwood Archives/UIG Universal Images, 16; North Wind Picture Archives: 21; NPS: Pony Express National Historic Trail, 26; The Pony Express National Museum, Inc., St. Joseph Missouri, Cover, 4, 11, 17, 22; Shutterstock (Design Elements): Itana, ixer, Miloje, Picsfive.

PRIMARY SOURCE BIBLIOGRAPHY
Page 17—Joseph J. Di Certo. *The Saga of the Pony Express.* Missoula, Montana: Mountain
        Press Publishing Company, 2002.
Page 18—"Pony Express: Romance vs. Reality." Smithsonian National Postal Museum.
        15 May 2015. http://postalmuseum.si.edu/exhibits/current/pony-express/
        pony-express-2.html
Page 20—Christopher Corbett. Orphans Preferred: *The Twisted Truth and Lasting Legacy
        of the Pony Express.* New York: Broadway Books, 2004.
Page 22—Jacqueline Lewin. "Heroes of the Pony Express." *American Cowboy.* 15 May 2015. www.
        americancowboy.com/article/heroes-pony-express-24260
Page 23—Carol Guthrie. *Pony Express: An Illustrated History.* Guilford, Conn.: Globe Pequot Press,
        2010.
Page 27—Christopher Reynolds. "On the trail of the Pony Express." *Los Angeles Times.*
        16 May 2010. 14 May 2015. http://articles.latimes.com/2010/may/16/travel/
        la-tr-ponyexpress-20100516/4

Printed in Canada.
052015   008825FRF15

TABLE OF CONTENTS

———— ◆ ————

1

OFF AND RUNNING

A crowd gathered along the dusty main street of
St. Joseph, Missouri. People huddled in the early evening
chill of a spring day in April 1860. They watched eagerly as
a thin young man climbed on a spirited horse.
A cannon boomed in the distance. The race
against time had begun!

FUN FACT

At first the western run of the
Pony Express ended at Sacramento,
California. From there mail went by
boat to San Francisco, California.
Later on riders sometimes carried
mail all the way to San Francisco.

The rider picked up a leather **mochila**, which had four pockets to carry letters. He threw the mochila over the horse's saddle.

Horse and rider raced to the bank of the Missouri River. A ferry boat waited there to carry them across the water. As the boat moved west, the crowd broke into applause. Some cheered. A few even cried.

Why were people so excited? It was the first leg of the first journey of the Pony Express. This new service promised to deliver mail from St. Joseph to Sacramento, California, in just 10 days. That would be more than twice as fast as what until then was the best service, offered by stagecoach.

> **mochila**—a specially designed lightweight leather bag used by the Pony Express to carry the mail

To meet the deadline, a series of riders would have to cover nearly 2,000 miles (3,219 kilometers) through what are now eight states. They had to cross **plains** and deserts. They faced steep mountains and swift rivers. They braved dangerous weather, including bone-chilling cold.

Riders also had to pass through the lands of many American Indian tribes. Some tribes were friendly. Others were **hostile**, angered by white settlers moving onto their land. The journey promised adventure—and danger.

> **plain**—a large, flat area of land with few trees
> **hostile**—unfriendly or angry

Few written records of the Pony Express remain. Historians argue about who made that first ride on April 3, 1860. No one knows who made the first ride, but everyone agrees on one thing. The Pony Express became a legend, and its legend kept growing over the years.

⚬⚬ FUN FACT ⚬⚬

The Pony Express route passed through the present states of Missouri, Kansas, Nebraska, Wyoming, Colorado, Utah, Nevada, and California.

WE WANT MAIL!

Delivering mail to the West faster had grown in importance. James Marshall discovered gold in California in 1848. Thousands of gold seekers traveled west hoping to get rich. Mining camps and cities sprang up everywhere. Miners and settlers wanted news from back home.

Providing that news presented a challenge. There was no Internet. There were no telephones, televisions, or radios. Newspapers and mail were the only way to carry news west. And there was no easy way to deliver it.

FUN FACT

Some men made their fortune carrying mail to men in mining communities. Miners paid Alexander Todd up to $16 per letter in gold dust to bring their mail to them. Todd made far more money than most of the miners and had a much easier life.

Workers return to a California gold mine after eating dinner.

Some people saw a chance to make money. In 1851 George Chorpenning and Absalom Woodward **contracted** with the U.S. government to carry mail between Sacramento and Salt Lake City, Utah. They used mules and horses to haul letters. Woodward was killed by American Indians during a run. Chorpenning was injured. Overland mail service to the West remained a problem.

contract—to enter into a legal agreement

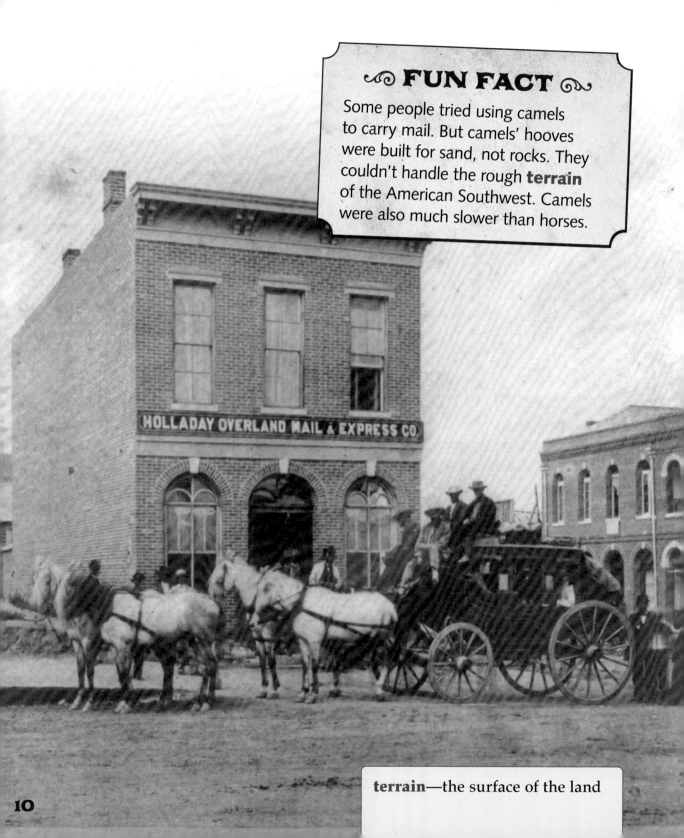

HOLLADAY OVERLAND MAIL & EXPRESS CO.

terrain—the surface of the land

Some mail traveled by steamship, but the water routes took weeks or even months. About 75,000 Californians signed a petition in 1856 asking the government for better mail service. Soon the Overland Mail Company got a government contract to carry mail by stagecoach. Their looping Southern Route covered roughly 2,800 miles (4,506 km). But it still took more than three weeks for mail to reach San Francisco from Missouri.

William Russell and his partners, Alexander Majors and William Waddell, ran the largest freight company in the West. In 1859 U.S. Senator William Gwin of California complained to Russell about slow mail service. Russell and his partners then decided to expand their service by carrying mail. They planned to use a straighter route than the Overland Company had, and a different delivery method—horses. The Pony Express was born.

Alexander Majors

William H. Russell

William B. Waddell

CHAPTER

3

SETTING
THE STAGE

The partners called their new business the Central
Overland California & Pike's Peak Express Company.
Most people simply called it the Pony Express. Their Central
Route followed the same path west that some settlers and
miners had taken since the California Gold Rush began.
Just under 2,000 miles (3,219 km), this route would cut days
from the delivery time for mail.

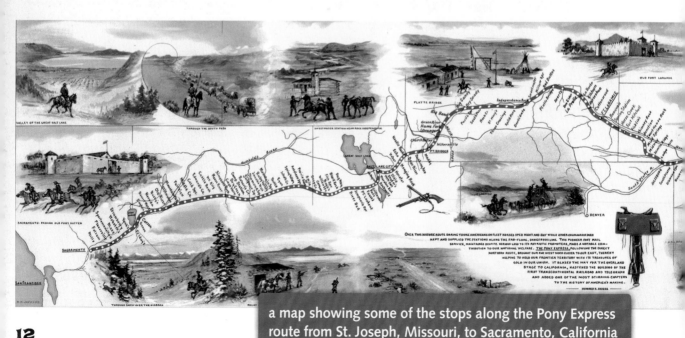

a map showing some of the stops along the Pony Express
route from St. Joseph, Missouri, to Sacramento, California

The first overland mail route to California traveled through southern states and territories. The Pony Express ran its Central Route through northern-leaning states and territories. When the **Civil War** began, the U.S. government didn't want to send mail through southern states. If the Pony Express had used a route through the South, Confederate forces may have tried to stop it.

Still, few people thought the Pony Express would succeed. The route crossed mountains, rivers, and deserts. Winter snowstorms and spring floods might prevent delivery. Riders also needed to cross land claimed by many American Indian tribes. Some of these tribes were warlike. How could lone riders get through?

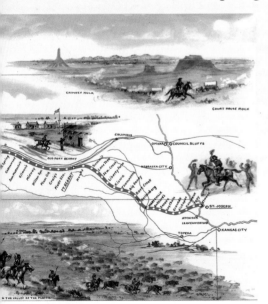

∾ FUN FACT ∾

On January 24, 1848, a carpenter working at a mill in northern California found two gold nuggets. The discovery led to the California Gold Rush.

THE POLITICS OF MAIL

In the 1850s the United States was divided over the issue of slavery. Southern states supported slavery. Northern states opposed it. California joined the Union as a free state in 1850. Still, there were many people from the South who had moved to California. The U.S. government believed that providing effective mail service to California could help make sure that the state remained loyal to the Union.

Civil War—(1861–1865) the battle between states in the North and South that led to the end of slavery in the United States

The company set up more than 150 stations along the route. Stations stood about 10 to 15 miles (16 to 24 km) apart. Under good conditions riders could cover that distance in an hour. At each station a rider would get a fresh horse. After about 80 to 100 miles (129 to 161 km), a new rider would take over.

A rider takes off on a fresh horse after a stop at a station.

Most stations were dirty, lonely places. Station keepers kept fresh horses ready. They provided food for the riders. Sometimes other travelers stopped on their way west. But most of the time the station keepers were alone. Sometimes they battled hostile American Indians.

The company split the vast trail into five sections. It hired a **superintendent** to manage each section. The superintendent made sure stations in his section were properly staffed and that fresh horses were always ready for the riders.

People wondered how the Pony Express could make money. Running such a service would be expensive. Income from carrying letters could never cover all the costs. But the owners had a plan. They hoped to get a million dollar mail contract from the federal government (worth about $29 million today). They could afford to lose some money at first—if the contract came through.

ꙮ FUN FACT ꙮ

At first the Pony Express charged $5 per half ounce (14 grams). In today's money that comes to about $140! That cost was later reduced to $2.50 when thinner paper was developed. Sending the same letter by boat cost only 10 cents, but delivery took months.

superintendent—a person who directs or manages an organization

CHAPTER 4

HORSES AND RIDERS

Now came the most important part—buying at least 400 horses and hiring 80 riders. The horses needed to be fast enough to outrun danger. They had to be strong enough to run through snow and swim across rivers. For the eastern part of the ride, the company bought horses from Kentucky. Further west they used **mustangs** from California.

∽ FUN FACT ∾

The Pony Express never used any ponies. The service used fast and sturdy horses. Sometimes they used mules for really rough terrain.

Billy Johnson rode for the Pony Express. He later worked for Buffalo Bill's Wild West show. He showed how Pony Express riders quickly changed horses.

Riders had to be expert horsemen. Alexander Majors later recalled wanting thin, **wiry** pony riders. Riders earned between $100 and $150 each month. They also received free room and board. That was excellent pay in those days.

The average Pony Express rider was around 21 years old. The oldest was likely in his 40s. No one knows for sure the age of the youngest rider. "Broncho Charlie" Miller claimed years later that he rode for the Pony Express at age 11. Many historians doubt that he was in the Pony Express at all.

Men Wanted!!

THE UNDERSIGNED WISHES TO

hire ten or a dozen men familiar with the management of horses, as hostlers or riders on the Overland Express Route via Salt Lake City. Wages, $50 per month and found. I may be found at the St. George Hotel Sunday, Monday and Tuesday

William W. Finney,

Agent for the Central Overland and Pikes Peak Express Company

mustang—a wild horse found mostly on the western plains of the United States
wiry—lean and tough

Riders and their horses acted as a team. Sometimes tired riders fell asleep in the saddle. Their horses simply kept going to the next relay stations. If a horse got injured along the way, the rider carried the mail by foot to the next station.

Riders sometimes blew a horn as they approached a station. Often they didn't bother. The station keepers could hear the sound of hoofbeats almost as far off as the horn. Riders raced into the station in a cloud of dust. The station keeper had a fresh horse saddled and ready. The rider slung the mochila onto the saddle. Sometimes he grabbed a bite to eat. Most stops took less than two minutes.

> ### ✑ FUN FACT ✑
> Pony Express riders had to take an oath not to fight with other employees, drink alcohol, or swear.

Riders spent long hours in the saddle and faced many dangers. They might get trampled by a herd of **stampeding** bison. They might have to outrun hostile American Indians. Even if all went smoothly, they finished their shifts stiff and sore from their hard rides. Few riders served throughout the entire time of the Pony Express. But nearly all riders had exciting stories to tell.

Pony Express riders were sometimes chased by hostile American Indians.

stampede—a sudden wild rush of a frightened herd of animals

CHAPTER 5

DANGER AND DARING

Few records were kept regarding Pony Express riders. That's one reason so many legends arose. No one could disprove them. But one thing is certain. The brave Pony Express riders had many adventures and faced many dangers. History shows that the Paiutes were at war with settlers and soldiers along the Pony Express route. When riders said they had tangled with or escaped hostile Paiutes, they were likely telling the truth. Sometimes they even had scars to show. We also know that some riders lost their lives in the line of duty. One rider died when his horse fell on him. Another was killed while trying to cross a river. A third rider froze to death. A fourth never reached his destination and was never found.

Pony Express Rider William Campbell said, "Riding express had more hard work than fun in it. We got exciting adventures [at] times to help keep things more interesting.... It took sheer grit and endurance at times to carry the mail through."

A Pony Express rider crosses a mountain during a snowstorm.

According to some accounts, Robert "Pony Bob" Haslam had two of the most thrilling Pony Express runs. In the spring of 1860, he rode about 360 miles (579 km) through the middle of Paiute raids. The raids left a Pony Express station destroyed and three station keepers dead. At one point the rider who was supposed to replace Haslam refused to ride into such danger. Haslam took his place and simply kept riding.

Haslam also was part of the team carrying news to the West of Abraham Lincoln's election as president in November 1860. This time Haslam ran into a Paiute war party. He later described his adventure to a newspaper reporter. "Look at these five front teeth," he said. "They were knocked out clean…. My jaw was fractured and I got another arrow through my left arm." Despite his injuries Haslam escaped and reached the next station.

"Pony Bob" Haslam

Snowstorms were hard on riders and their horses. Sometimes the snow was so deep, it was hard to know where the road was.

Weather posed danger too. Richard Cleve recalled riding through "one of the worst blizzards that I ever saw" in Nebraska in early 1861. The snow was so deep he couldn't find the road. The temperature reached -40 degrees Fahrenheit (-40 degrees Celsius). Finding that his relief rider was ill, Cleve rode a double shift. In all, he covered 150 miles (241 km) in 36 hours.

These stories come from the Pony Express riders themselves. Might they have exaggerated to make their stories even more thrilling? Maybe. We can't say for sure. No one can deny, however, that they rode through extreme conditions and faced real dangers.

THE LEGEND
LIVES ON

Big changes came to both the United States and the Pony Express in 1861. In March the Pony Express carried the text of Lincoln's **Inaugural Address** from Nebraska to California in the record time of 7 days and 17 hours. On April 12 the Civil War began.

Telegraph lines were built to connect the United States from coast to coast.

✿ FUN FACT ✿

Only one mochila was ever lost. A letter from it was found two years later and delivered.

Despite receiving some government funding, the Pony Express remained deep in debt. It seemed unclear how much longer the Pony Express could continue.

Then came news of progress that would doom the Pony Express. A recent invention called the **telegraph** allowed messages to travel as coded electronic signals over a wire strung between wooden poles.

Inaugural Address—the speech a president gives when he or she is sworn into office
telegraph—a system of sending messages over long distances that used wires and electrical signals

TWO FAMOUS BILLS

Two of the most famous men associated with the Pony Express were both named Bill—"Wild Bill" Hickok and "Buffalo Bill" Cody. Hickok worked at a Pony Express station. He later became one of the West's most famous **marshals**. Many experts doubt Cody's claim that he was a Pony Express rider. After becoming a famous buffalo hunter, he created Buffalo Bill's Wild West Show. He toured the United States and Europe with his show. He even performed for Queen Victoria of England. His show helped build the legend of the Pony Express.

PONY EXPRESS

THIS MEMORIAL IS THE PROPERTY OF THE STATE OF COLORADO

DUE NORTH 1235 FEET IS THE ORIGINAL SITE OF

OLD JULESBURG

NAMED FOR JULES BENI WHOSE TRADING POST WAS ESTABLISHED AT THE "UPPER CROSSING" OF THE PLATTE PRIOR TO 1860. JUNCTION OF OREGON AND OVERLAND TRAILS. PONY EXPRESS STATION, 1860-61. OVERLAND STAGE STATION, 1859-65. BURNED IN INDIAN RAID, FEB. 2, 1865.

ERECTED BY THE STATE HISTORICAL SOCIETY OF COLORADO FROM THE MRS. J. N. HALL FOUNDATION AND BY CITIZENS OF SEDGWICK COUNTY, COLORADO 1931

marshal—an officer of a federal court who has duties similar to those of a sheriff

Over time telegraph lines extended all the way west to California. By October 1861 messages could travel from New York to San Francisco in minutes by telegraph. That included the time it took an operator to decode the message.

Just 18 months after it began, the Pony Express closed. The final mail messages were delivered on November 20.

Many mourned the end of the Pony Express. *The Sacramento Bee* wrote, "Our little friend, the Pony, is to run no more…. Farewell … swift-footed messenger."

As a business the Pony Express failed. But its legend continued to grow as a symbol of western adventure. People loved to hear stories about its riders and the dangers they faced. Through Buffalo Bill's Wild West Show, people across the world got a glimpse of how the Pony Express worked.

a poster for Buffalo's Bill's Wild West show

ꙮ FUN FACT ꙮ

During its 18 months in business, the Pony Express carried almost 35,000 pieces of mail.

Over time the facts and legends about the Pony Express started to blend together. We may never know whether all of the stories about the Pony Express and its riders are true. In the end, maybe it doesn't matter. It represents an exciting time in the history of the United States.

TIMELINE

1848
James Marshall discovers gold in California. Within a year, thousands of people went west in search of riches.

1853
The firm of Waddell & Russell is founded. They are later joined by Majors. Soon they have built one of the largest freight firms in the West.

1856
About 75,000 people in California sign a petition demanding better mail service to California.

April 3, 1860
The first Pony Express rider leaves Missouri. The mail arrives in California 10 days later. Meanwhile a rider leaves California heading east.

1848

1860

1850
California becomes a U.S. state.

1851
The U.S. government offers a contract to two men to carry mail from Salt Lake City, Utah, to Sacramento, California, and back again. One partner is killed by American Indians. The other is badly wounded.

1857
The Overland Mail Company begins carrying mail from Missouri to California by stagecoach. Their Southern Route takes more than three weeks to complete.

1859
Senator William Gwin of California complains to William Russell about mail service. Russell forms the idea of a Pony Express service across the straighter Central Route.

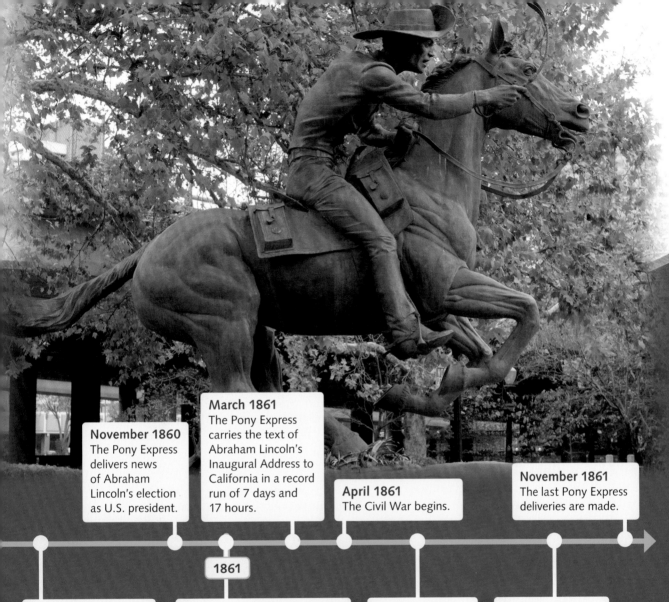

November 1860
The Pony Express delivers news of Abraham Lincoln's election as U.S. president.

March 1861
The Pony Express carries the text of Abraham Lincoln's Inaugural Address to California in a record run of 7 days and 17 hours.

April 1861
The Civil War begins.

November 1861
The last Pony Express deliveries are made.

1861

May and June 1860
Paiute raids disrupt the Pony Express.

January and February 1861
Several southern states secede from the Union.

Summer, 1861
Work begins to run a telegraph connection across the United States.

October 1861
The telegraph route is completed, and the Pony Express announces that it is closing.

GLOSSARY

Civil War (SIV-il WOR)—(1861–1865) the battle between states in the North and South that led to the end of slavery in the United States

contract (KAHN-trakt)—to enter into a legal agreement

hostile (HOSS-tuhl)—unfriendly or angry

Inaugural Address (in-AW-gyuh-ruhl uh-DRESS)—the speech a president gives when he or she is sworn into office

marshal (MAR-shul)—an officer of a federal court who has duties similar to those of a sheriff

mochila (mo-CHI-luh)—a specially designed lightweight leather bag used by the Pony Express to carry the mail.

mustang (MUHSS-tang)—a wild horse found mostly on the western plains of the United States

plain (PLAYN)—a large, flat area of land with few trees

stampede (stam-PEED)—a sudden wild rush of a frightened herd of animals

superintendent (soo-pur-in-TEN-duhnt)—a person who directs or manages an organization

telegraph (TEL-uh-graf)—a system of sending messages over long distances that used wires and electrical signals

terrain (tuh-RAYN)—the surface of the land

wiry (WYE-ree)—lean and tough

READ MORE

Jeffrey, Gary. *The Pony Express.* A Graphic History of the American West. New York: Gareth Stevens Pub., 2012.

Kay, Verla. *Whatever Happened to the Pony Express?* New York: G.P. Putnam's Sons, 2010.

Marsh, Carole. *Galloping West with the Pony Express.* American Milestones. Peachtree City, Ga.: Gallopade International, 2010.

O'Hearn, Michael. *The El Dorado Map.* North Mankato, Minn.: Stone Arch Books, 2015.

Ratliff, Tom. *You Wouldn't Want to Be a Pony Express Rider!: A Dusty, Thankless Job You'd Rather Not Do.* You Wouldn't Want to—. New York: Franklin Watts, 2012.

Savage, Jeff. *Daring Pony Express Riders: True Tales of the Wild West.* New York: Enslow Publishers, Inc., 2012.

INTERNET SITES

FactHound offers a safe, fun way to find Internet sites related to this book. All of the sites on FactHound have been researched by our staff.

Here's all you do:

Visit *www.facthound.com*

Type in this code: 9781491448960

 Check out projects, games and lots more at **www.capstonekids.com**

CRITICAL THINKING USING THE COMMON CORE

1. How does the author support the idea that Pony Express riders faced danger and difficulties with every run? (Key Ideas and Details)

2. How does the timeline on pages 28 and 29 help you better understand the Pony Express as it related to other historical events in the 1850s and early 1860s? (Integration of Knowledge and Ideas)

3. Several of the stories and quotes in this book come from eyewitness accounts by the Pony Express riders themselves. In many cases, however, there was no one else present to support or deny these accounts. How are these personal memories different from the straightforward, factual information presented in other parts of the book? (Craft and Structure)

INDEX